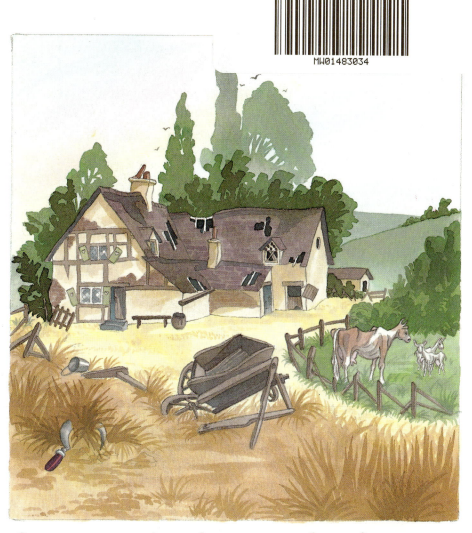

Once upon a time there was a lazy farmer. The farmer's name was Eric. Look at Eric's farm. His fields are full of weeds. His cows and goats are hungry, and his house is falling down.

Look at Eric's family. His wife and children work hard, but there is no food to eat. Their clothes are old and they are unhappy. The family is very poor.

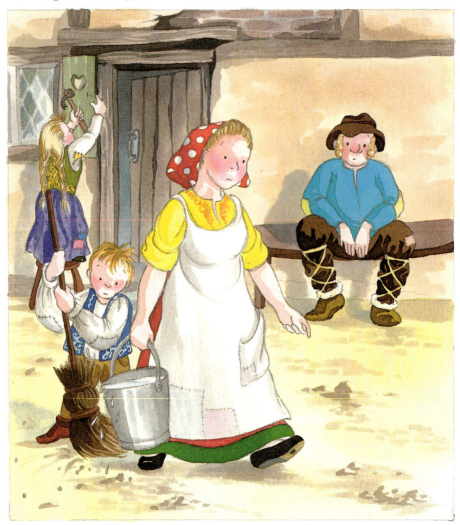

Eric: Oh, dear. I'm very hungry. Can I have something to eat please, Anna?

Anna: No, you can't. There's no food. Go out and work.

Eric: I can't work. I'm hungry and I'm tired too.

Anna: You're lazy and you owe people money. Go out and work. Go on, get out!

Eric: What can I do now? I don't like work.
I want to sit under this tree and sleep.
Ah, that's nice. It's cool here. Oh!
What's this? It's an old flute. I like
playing the flute. Hey, this flute is great!

4

Eric: Good morning.
Woman: Good morning, Eric. How are you?
Eric: I'm tired and I'm hungry. Do you
have any food in your basket?
Woman: Yes, I have some bread, some apples,
some cheese and a lovely cake.

5

Eric: Fantastic! Give me the cake, the apples and the cheese, please.

Woman: All right. You can have the food. But I want some money for it.

Eric: I'm sorry. I don't have any money. But you can have this flute.

Woman: I don't want your flute. I want money for my food.

Eric: But it's a very good flute. Listen.

Woman: Help! Help! I can't stop dancing.

Eric: Hey! This flute is magic.
Come on, dance! Faster, faster!

Woman: Oh, please stop playing your flute.
You can have all my food. I don't
want any money. Please stop.

Eric: OK. Thanks very much for the food.
You can go now.

Woman: You're a wicked man, Eric. You
have all my food and I don't have
any money.

Eric: Mm ... This cake is lovely. The apples and oranges are delicious. And this flute is fantastic. I play it and people can't stop dancing. Then they give me what I want. Ha, ha! Why work now?

8

Eric: Good morning.

Boy: Good morning.

Eric: Those are very fine goats. Can I have them, please?

Boy: Yes, but I want some money for them.

Eric: I'm sorry, I don't have any money. But you can have this flute.

Boy: I don't want your flute. I want money for my goats.

Eric: But it's a very good flute. Listen.

Boy: Help! Help! I can't stop dancing.

Eric: Come on, dance! Faster, faster!

Boy: Please stop playing your flute. You can have all my goats. Take them.

Eric: Thanks very much. You can go now.

Boy: You're a wicked man. You have all my goats and I don't have any money.

Eric: Good morning, sir.

Man: Good morning.

Eric: I'm very poor, sir. Please give me some money.

Man: You aren't poor. You have food in that basket and you have all these goats.

Eric: Give me some money or hear my flute.

Man: I don't want to hear your flute.

Man: Help! Help! I can't stop dancing.

Eric: Come on, dance or give me your money.

Man: Please stop playing your flute. You
can have all my money. Take it. Take it.

Eric: Thanks very much. You can go now.

Man: You're a wicked man. You have all my
money and I have nothing.

Eric: Hello, Anna. Look! I have a basket of
food, all these goats and lots of money.

Anna: How did you get all this?

Eric: With this flute. I found it. When I play
it people dance and dance and dance.
They can't stop. Then they give me
anything I want.

Anna: That's wicked, Eric. It's dishonest.
We must give these things back.

Anna: That's a terrible flute. Throw it away.

  Eric: Don't say that, Anna. It's a wonderful flute. We can get food and money and goats and cows with it.

Anna: You're a lazy, dishonest man. You must work for our food and money and animals. Don't cheat people with this flute. Give it to me. I want to throw it on the fire.

  Eric: Stop! Don't throw it on the fire. Play it. It's really good.

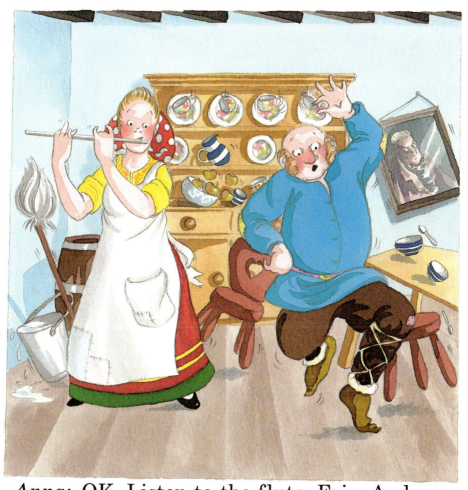

Anna: OK. Listen to the flute, Eric. And
dance. Come on, dance! Faster, faster!

Eric: Help! Help! I can't stop dancing.
Please stop playing the flute, Anna.

Anna: Do you want to work or dance, Eric?

Eric: I want to work hard. Please stop, Anna.

Look at Eric's farm now. The fields are full of animals. The animals have food to eat. Anna and the children are happy. Eric works hard. But the flute is never far from Anna!